EMBRACE
YOUR SUCCESS

8 Tools to Improve the Quality of Your Life

By Ana Barreto

BOOKS BY ANA BARRETO

Women, Rice, and Beans: Discover Wisdom in Ordinary Moments
Self-Trust: A Healing Practice for Women Who Do Too Much
There is a Higher Power Within: 28 Meditation Prompts to Find Peace &
Happiness Within
The Nine Powers of Women: Awakening the Divine Feminine Within

PROGRAMS BY ANA BARRETO

Quantum Healing Through the Chakras
Clear Your Fear of Success
Finding a Greater Wellbeing in a Busy World with Meditation
Timefulness: The Art of Aligning Time with Purpose
Making Space for a Loving Relationship
Discover Your Purpose & Mission
A Crash Course in Confidence

HOW TO CONNECT ONLINE:

Visit http://www.ana-barreto.com for meditations,
classes, and inspirational content
Like my page on Facebook: @ana1barreto
Follow me on Instagram: @ana1barreto
Follow me on Twitter: @ana1barreto
Follow me on Pinterest: @ana1barreto
Send your comments, questions, and concerns to ana@ana-barreto.com

1st Edition, March 2024
ISBN-13: 979-8-9876158-6-7
Blue Hudson Group, Albany, NY

All photos are by Ana Barreto, except for the ones on pages 3 and 15, which
are by Anatercia Chaves. Photos on the back cover and page 19 are by Tyiesha
Ford.

For Teca

CONTENTS

LEAVING THE FLOCK BEHIND

Soaring high above the confines of self-doubt, the awakened spirit embraced its true nature, leaving the limitations of the flock behind.

Once upon a time, in a small village nestled between rolling hills, there lived a farmer. One spring morning, while collecting eggs from his henhouse, the farmer stumbled upon a large, speckled egg that stood out from the rest. Curious, he carefully picked it up and decided to place it among the eggs in the chicken coop.

Weeks passed, and one by one, the eggs hatched, filling the coop with chirps and cheeps. Among the fluffy chicks was the egg the farmer found, but instead of hatching into a chick, it revealed a majestic eagle.

Unaware of its true identity, the eagle was raised alongside the chickens, pecking at the grain and scratching in the dirt just like its feathered companions.

Years went by, and the eagle grew accustomed to its life amongst the chickens, never questioning its place in the world. It clucked, clambered, and flew short distances just like the rest. The eagle was content in its routine.

One day, as the eagle pecked at the ground, it noticed a shadow gliding gracefully across the sky. Looking up, the eagle saw a magnificent creature with broad wings soaring effortlessly above. Mesmerized, the eagle watched as the majestic bird danced with the clouds, feeling excitement deep within its soul.

Intrigued, the eagle approached the other chickens, asking about the magnificent bird in the sky. The chickens chuckled and dismissed the eagle's curiosity: "That is the king of the sky. They belong up there."

"Why can't we fly like them?" insisted the eagle.

They looked at each other and laughed, "We belong on the ground." Said one of the chickens. "Those birds don't mingle with us," Another continued.

But days went by, and the eagle couldn't shake the longing it felt watching the soaring bird. One day, it tried to spread its wings, but the chickens corrected him right away. "You are no eagle! Stop this nonsense."

Each time the eagle talked about the soaring bird in the sky, the chickens shut it down or dismissed it.

Eventually, the eagle was convinced and spent his days being a chicken. He died as a chicken, never using its powerful wings or soaring to its potential for courage, determination, and boundless freedom.

* * *

Welcome to your journey of awakening to your true potential, my dear eagle.

You have been called to this moment. You have felt a stirring deep within, a longing to fully step into your light and share your success with the world. By now, you have realized that you are not a chicken, and it's time to soar to your highest potential.

Though this path is often filled with fear, doubt, busyness, and habits that distract you, this one will lead you to profound joy, purpose, and freedom.

When I first began sensing this call, I resisted it with all my might. My environment didn't support it. I was a divorced mother of two young children, struggling to balance all of my home and work responsibilities while working on myself. My life felt like a whirlwind I could barely keep up with. I was constantly exhausted, impatient, and on edge. Deep down, I sensed something was missing. But I didn't know how to slow down enough to find it.

I had always been fiercely independent and prided myself on handling everything alone. Though my girlfriends loved me, I kept them at a distance and rarely asked for help. I was helping everyone. I mistakenly equated needing support with failure or weakness. I was also a perfectionist who feared I could never live up to the high standards I'd internalized.

For years, I pushed down my feelings of sadness, frustration, longing, and anger. I survived on coffee, adrenaline, and sheer willpower, falsely believing this hustle was the requirement for a "superwoman." But at night, anxieties and resentments would dance in my head, stealing precious rest and reminding me that my cape waited for me in the morning. My body's exhaustion began manifesting as headaches and developed into migraines. Still, I carried on, not knowing any other way.

The turning point came on the morning after my 42nd birthday when I awoke feeling decades older than forty, hollow, and numb. Instead of being excited for the new year ahead, I could barely drag myself out of bed. My mind drowned in negative self-talk about how little I had accomplished and how mediocre my life felt compared to my expectations. On top of that, I had a decision to make since my boyfriend had shown up three hours late and high the night before. It was my birthday dinner on a school night when my children had to go to bed early.

Finally, the tears I had bottled up for years burst forth. I took my children to school, called out, and cried deeply for hours, allowing myself to feel and release the pent-up sadness, anger, and fear I'd long denied myself. In my raw heartache, I knew something had to fundamentally change. That's the seed of change: rock bottom.

HOW DID I GET THERE?

It started in Rio de Janeiro, Brazil. I know well the story of my birth because my mother told it multiple times. It was an impossible holiday. There were parades in the streets of Rio on a five-day holiday weekend celebrating Independence Day. All the stores were closed, people were at the beach, and my mother felt on-and-off contractions despite the missing moon.

From the one-room apartment with a single window, my mother watched my dad go to a payphone to call the doctor. Doctor Nelson, who had already delivered my sister nineteen months earlier, sent my parents to the nearby hospital in Ipanema. He must have believed it was too early for delivery, and he didn't want to waste his time driving to the affordable hospital where my mother had been seen before.

After a short taxi ride, my parents arrived at the lobby dressed in red carpet, pristine white walls, and bright, humongous paintings. The nurses looked like television nurses wearing well-starched white uniforms. It was fancy! –my mother said.

One nurse took my mother to a regular exam room that was as fancy as the lobby. My mother was told to change into a patient gown and wait for the doctor, who hadn't arrived yet. She struggled to lie down on the hospital bed but didn't complain. The nurse examined my mother and pushed me back into the womb. My head was coming out. "You can't have the baby here," – said the nurse.

I didn't have the traditional new baby clothes to leave the hospital because my dad didn't have the money. The doctor rushed my mother out of the hospital because it was too expensive for my parents. I left with the nurse's thumbprint on the top of my head. And that's how I was born: unplanned and rushed.

My father got his act together, and soon, our family was able to move from a one-room apartment with three children to a two-bedroom apartment five houses from the beach in Governor's Island, which today houses the international airport in Rio. Three additional children were born in that apartment.

Things were good for a few years until they were no more. I don't remember when it changed. Money was tight, bills weren't paid, the electricity would be shut off from time to time, and Santa didn't come every Christmas. Some weeks, we didn't do grocery shopping. Other weeks, we received help from the church without my father's knowledge. He was too proud to receive assistance. Also, he didn't allow my mother to work, even though she had a profession and he couldn't afford his family. The little money I earned by giving guitar lessons in my teen years would be used to buy food from time to time.

Most of the time, I felt that I lived at the end of the world, where the good winds forgot to go. The moon seemed to agree with me every time we watched the last bus go by at 11:35 pm. It was quiet and pretty but too far from where I felt I belonged.

A person born on Independence Day must have freedom. I didn't have any, and neither did my mother. All decisions were made by my father, even simple ones like selecting the curtains or the flowers. On my fifteenth birthday, I told my mother that I couldn't wait to be eighteen years old to leave the house. And one week before I came of age, I did just that.

I had been offered a job as an international telephone operator in a four-star hotel in Copacabana Beach. I spoke enough English to communicate with the guests, who would place a breakfast order or request a wake-up call. My father prohibited me from taking the job because he believed that women who work in hotels are prostitutes.

Freedom came at a high price. Money was tight; I learned to live on Frosted Flake cereal and yogurt. I became an expert in dating for food; that's when you go out with a guy to have a meal.

One morning, when I was meditating, I had a dream-like vision. In this half-awake, half-sleep dream, I saw myself in America. I was speaking to people in English. In Rio, I didn't know what I was saying, but the people I was talking to in my vision understood me. When I came back from it, I realized I was going to New York, and four months later, I arrived at JFK. It was May 28th, 1988. A few days later, I recognized the location of my dream: Mamaroneck, NY.

The original plan was to come to New York for six months, earn some money, and see the guy who stopped calling, but this is another story. It has lasted 35 years so far as I write this manuscript. I had $1,000 in my purse, of which $460 of that was to be sent back to my brother, who lent me the money. I worked as a housekeeper, a babysitter, and a dog walker for a few years.

I didn't have enough money to attend college full-time, so I pursued a part-time education at Westchester Community College, paying out-of-state tuition while working 40 hours a week. I had influential teachers and mentors who encouraged me to find a way to continue my education, and so I did. I received a 50% scholarship from Marymount College, which was an all-girls college. Today, it is part of Fordham University in New York.

Those were the years when the seed of my mission found soil to grow. I learned about the history of women. And I became very passionate and curious to understand how women learned endurance. I already knew of women's strength and struggle. There were the lessons written on the walls I had to wash clean, along with the crayon drawings my younger brothers drew.

Growing up, women couldn't have bank accounts or own property without the approval of their fathers or husbands. Women hid their birth control pills from their husbands and community; they were discouraged from working, and they had no voice. Unhappy married women couldn't seek divorce because they couldn't afford it, and the risk of being marginalized was too high of a price to pay. So, I embarked on a path and discovered my mission to educate and support women to their greatness, but I didn't know what I was flowing toward until 2014.

In the beginning, my life didn't fully match my mission. I got married, had two children, earned an MBA, got divorced, landed my dream job, made great money, and then later hated my dream job. I worked constantly and barely spent time with my children. I couldn't wait for them to grow up. Most of the time, I felt guilty, angry, and quietly regretful. I felt unhappy without knowing because we had learned not to talk about it. I had migraines every other week that put me in bed for 24 hours. I was exhausted. I planned my Saturday naps on Wednesdays. Do you know what TGIF is? Mine was TGIM – Thank God It's Monday. I couldn't wait for Mondays because I worked more on Saturdays and Sundays. I crammed my family obligations on the weekends.

The "shoulds" are heavy burdens on the shoulders of anyone who allows their lives to pass by. I ate "should" for breakfast, lunch, and dinner. Mostly, my "shoulds" were to be a better mother, a better boss, a better daughter, a better housekeeper, and a better woman. Work distracted my "should." So, I was never slowed down enough to realize my shadow lived my life. I was just a bystander in my life. I was working on the next thing, the next project, or the next win. But the Universe has big plans for everyone. And the way the Universe got my attention was by putting me in bed sick.

During one of the sick days, I knew I hit bottom. I was so tired of the ups and downs, and I began to search for a better way to live. I was already studying Feng Shui, spirituality, and metaphysics. I began to meditate more consistently and slowed down to actually live. Meditation got me to slow down enough to pay attention and be quiet enough to hear the whispers of my soul.

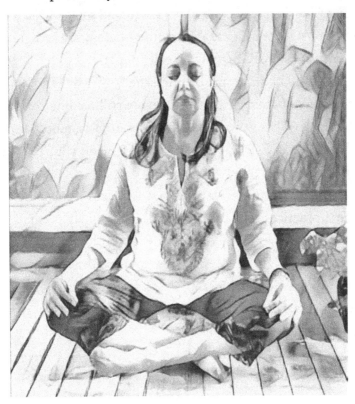

So, today, I will share with you my eight easy tools to improve the quality of your daily life that I received during meditation. This was an inspirational talk I published a few years back and received great feedback. I originally published it for women and received feedback that men could benefit from the tools, too.

I want to support you in releasing behaviors that hold you back from being your true self and from doing the things you were meant to share with the world. These tools worked for me and many people.

These tools are not in any order of importance. Some of you will feel these insights at your core, and some of you will recognize these insights are for others before you recognize them for yourself. Before you call your friend to tell them to read the book, stop. This message is for you. This time is about you and you alone. If you are still reading this far, that means that you are searching for answers, too, and the Universe got your attention. So, I commend you. You are on your way.

One big warning: As you start incorporating some of these practices into your life, things are likely to change rapidly. You may be called to quit your job, leave a relationship, lose weight, move to a new house, or make amends with your past. Just breathe and embrace the changes you will be creating. It is coming at the right time. You were born an eagle; It's time to soar.

The Process

Although I received these tools in meditation, practicing them didn't happen all at once. I fought many of them at first. But the Universe didn't give up on me and slowly showed me how to nurture the seeds of my rebirth. I discovered the incredible power of creating a daily morning ritual centered on meditation, affirmation, and Gratitude so my soul could emerge. I began carving out non-negotiable me-time. I faced my fears about asking loved ones for help. I made space for rest, play, and creativity that had long been missing. My soul was starving for me. Chances are your soul is starving for you, too.

Have compassion towards your own imperfect progress. These tools helped me gradually shed old limiting beliefs about my self-worth and capabilities. You can, too.

I used to belong to the "Blame Club," which is free to join and drains your time, heart, inspiration, and light. Membership only requires you to blame someone and anything, and even God, for the troubles you created. I realized so clearly that the negative self-talk did not reflect reality. I began trusting the wisdom of my intuition over the fickle mind. I started saying yes to opportunities I had previously passed up. And they were still waiting for me.

Everything you want is already here.
You must be willing to see it.

The more love, approval, and security I gave myself through this awakening process, the more energy I discovered to share my talents. It reignited my passion for music, art, poetry, travel, and more.

The eight tools in the chapters ahead offer you pathways to your own awakening toward your success. They guide you to unlock your full potential so you can fearlessly walk the path of your destiny. As you incorporate these practices into your daily life, you will shed old limiting beliefs and begin to create the reality of your dreams. Get ready to fall in love with yourself and your life in a whole new way.

The journey begins within. There is plenty of light. Your inner light has been waiting for you to strengthen its flames; just open your inner eyes. If you don't know your purpose, be willing to see it now with no judgment or outside expectations. Trust yourself like you never did before. Trust. Trust those goosebumps, also called "God-bumps." Trust that gut sensation, the inner smile of confidence; just trust. The world needs your light; even though you have an eternity to share your talents, it doesn't have to take that long.

CHAPTER 1:

CREATE A SACRED SPACE

> Men have caves;
> Women have sacred spaces.

A man was walking face down in the park across the street from his home. He walked slowly and used his feet to move the grass from side to side. His neighbor watched him for a while and decided to cross the street and offer assistance. Did you lose something? Asked the neighbor
"I lost my keys."
The neighbor began to walk around looking for the keys to help.
After fifteen minutes, the neighbor asked:
"Are you sure you lost the keys here in the park?"
"No, I lost them in my house, but there is more light here."

People are often looking for answers outside, in the world, when all the answers they seek lay within. People need a sacred space of their own. And women need it mostly.

Why? Because everyone needs time to go within. I say, create the space, and you will make the time to use it.

Everyone needs time to regenerate and separate themselves from the things they do and the people they support that deplete their energy. You need to create a space so you can make the time to retreat, recharge your energy, and revive your spirit.

An activity that does not bring you enthusiasm takes energy away from you. If you don't enjoy doing laundry but do it anyway, the task will deplete your energy. If you don't like your job, going to work will take energy away from you. Your children also drain your energy, especially when you work all day, are physically tired, and need your undivided attention. When that happens, you dig deep into yourself and release the reservoir that is meant to keep you healthy. Women learned to do that so well, and they work out of their reserve until there is no more.

Of course, laundry, jobs, and children don't have to deplete our energy. It is the thoughts we have about them that create drainage. Our lives are full of responsibilities that we may not always be thrilled to complete, but we choose to do it. To offset that, you need to make time to feed your spirit. Creating a space will allow time for yourself. Men have caves, and women have sacred spaces.

Your sacred space can exist in any area of your home. It can be your bedroom, a corner of your bedroom, your home office, or an area in the living room. All you need to do is find it, clean it, clear it, and bless it to make it yours. Make the space beautiful because you deserve it. Make it inviting, use colors that you adore, and fill it with objects that bring you joy and centeredness.

Make the space an area that you will want to go to meditate, pray, write, relax, read, knit, reflect, retreat from the world, or do essentially any activity that nurtures your body, mind, and spirit.

The beauty of space, combined with time spent on self-nurturing activities, tells the Universe that you are precious and deserve peace, joy, and restoration.

Carving out a corner of your home as a sacred sanctuary or your cave devoted solely to nourishing yourself is profoundly powerful medicine. Your sacred space is a physical representation of honoring your self-worth. It sends a clear message to the Universe that you are precious and deserving of peace, restoration, and joy. This space becomes a haven from the stress of everyday life, a place to quiet your mind and reconnect with your essence.

When I first read about creating a sacred space in my 20s, I'll admit I rolled my eyes a bit at the idea. My tiny one-room apartment in Manhattan with a shared hallway bathroom that I shared with my best friend could barely contain the few furnishings we found on garbage days, let alone set aside an entire corner just for me. I marveled when my roommate wasn't home so I could have quiet time. The concept sounded nice but didn't seem realistic. If this is the case, keep reading, as I have a few solutions for you.

After my divorce, my bedroom became my sacred space. Later on, I had an office, and these days, my children are out of the house, and I find a few corners in my home. I realized just how much I needed to devote space to nourish myself.

This principle of a sacred space is not new. Virginia Woolf wrote about A Room of One's Own in 1929 to have the space and resources to write as a woman. Eleanor Roosevelt also shared her relief when she built her house after living in her mother-in-law's home for forty-two years. She called it "coming home."

Louisa May Alcott had a corner of her own. Her father built her a small wooden desk circa 1877 at her father's house in Concord, Massachusetts. The desk was the sacred space where she wrote the book "Little Women."

Soul's Appointment

People need a chair, desk, corner, room, or a space of their own to pray, laugh, cry, meditate, retreat, sleep, read, cook, decorate, mature, and be intoxicated with their own soul's scent. It's a space of self-rescue.

You don't need much room at all to create a sacred space with a huge impact. Choose a small area in your home that feels comforting, whether it's a corner of your bedroom or living room. Clear the clutter and thoroughly clean the space, opening windows to allow in fresh air and sunshine. Smudging with sage is a wonderful way to eliminate stagnant energy.

Next, bless your sacred space by lighting a candle, sprinkling holy water, or burning incense while setting the intention that this will be a profoundly healing, meditative place for you. Decorate it beautifully with items that feel nurturing, such as soft pillows, inspiring art, crystals, flowers, spiritual books, or whatever calls to your soul. I have a blanket, a pillow, and three shawls I love.

The key is making your sacred space so inviting that you eagerly look forward to retreating here. Schedule regular times to visit your sanctuary - even if just for 5 or 10 minutes - and honor these as soul appointments that replenish you. Build it, and you will be called to use it.

Activities to nourish yourself in your sacred space include:

- Meditation - Stilling your mind quiets inner turmoil and connects you to inner wisdom.

- Journaling - Expressing your thoughts and feelings has deep healing powers.

- Reading - Books can inspire profound shifts in consciousness.

- Solving problems – Reflecting while resting will open your mind to possibilities.

- Listening to music - Let soothing melodies wash away stress and uplift your energy.

- Creating art - Painting, drawing, or working with clay centers your spirit.

- Movement - Gentle yoga, dance, or stretching opens energy flow.

- Time with nature - Caring for plants or using natural objects for altarpieces is balancing

- Aromatherapy - Essential oils profoundly impact mood and energy.

Most importantly, your sacred space is a place to simply be, to set down the weight of the world, and rest in the stillness of the present moment. There, you can recharge your soul batteries so you have energy for your life's purpose and loved ones. When people nourish themselves, they become a divine force for good.

CHAPTER 2:

MEDITATE

> Meditation is the new "high."

Meditation is the medicine the world has been seeking. And I am not exaggerating.

Have you experienced a moment of such bliss that you don't want it to end? That's a state you can achieve in meditation without any drugs.

Meditation is the process of exiting thinking. Why do we need to stop thought? Our thoughts create our world, and we think too many negative thoughts that don't serve us. When we focus on our breath and stop thinking our habitual thoughts, peace, wisdom, and harmony become available to us.

We also increase our own vibration, and low-energy people, events, and things cannot get into our experience. We are able to see things through the eyes of the source, we feel the emotions that support our intentions, and our actions bring us closer to where we want to go.

Most often, I hear that people believe they don't know how to meditate or that they can't stop thinking. This is because they think that meditation is sitting still on the top of a mountain, with crossed legs, chanting like a monk. Although this is also meditation, there are other forms of meditation. Here is an easy meditation practice that you can start today with no effort.

When you first wake up in the morning, your eyes are still closed, and you are still deciding if you should get up or stay there. Stay. Feel the bed, feel the pillow against your skin, and take slow, deep, and long breaths.

Concentrate on your breath and begin relaxing parts of your body.

Relax your scalp, your forehead, and your eyes;

Relax your jaw, your neck, and your shoulders;

Relax your arms, hands, and fingers

Relax your upper back, lower back, and hips;

Relax your thighs, knees, calves, feet and toes.

Just by reading the above sentences, you had a very short meditation.

Your mind will wander during this time, thinking about the kids, the job, the relationship, and other life moments. When you have realized that you did wander, gently release the thoughts and just go back to concentrating on your breathing. Stay there for 5 minutes, but 8 minutes would be best.

Full disclosure. When you first start meditating, you don't feel much. You don't know what to feel or if you are doing it right, and that trips any meditator. Until one day, something happens. You don't know what it is, but it feels good. You get up and go about your day. A few days later, you try again, and nothing happens, but the next time you meditate, you feel really good again, and you want to do it more. The next time, you may feel inclined to meditate longer.

There are other ways. I strongly recommend that newbies start with guided meditations of 10 minutes or less. Find a voice and pace you like. You will appreciate more when the guided meditation has an intention, such as releasing anger, finding forgiveness, getting guidance, and more.

I personally recommend that you start with 5 minutes of a body scan meditation, just like the one you read above, and gradually increase your practice. When you are leaning to swim, you don't just jump in the deep end, right? Start slow.

You can also download a guided meditation from my website at www.ana-barreto.com/meditations. Or you can use apps such as Insight Timmer. You can find my meditations at http://insighttimer.com/anabarreto. Other teachers offer free guided meditations that will help you get started.

Meditation as a Practice

Meditation is one of the easiest ways for you to release unpleasant past experiences, unwanted emotions, parental conditioning, find self-love, forgiveness, and more.

Find a meditation practice that you like and do it in the morning whenever possible. Mornings are the most optimal time to reach high levels of consciousness. When you wake up in the morning, your brain is going from the delta brain waves – sleeping- into alpha brain waves – a flow state - which is the state where you are calm and creative and have an increased ability to absorb and retain information. In this state, you are likely to tap into your own world of knowledge and wisdom, also called your inner guidance.

People have received guidance in meditation that led them to discoveries, new jobs, new homes, investments, and other great wins. I, too, have been guided to take action while meditating.

Jack Canfield received the title of his book "Chicken Soup for the Soul" during meditation. The book series went on to sell more than 500 million copies in 43 languages. Oprah Winfrey said, "I give myself twenty minutes in the morning, twenty minutes in the evening. Knowing that stillness is the space where all creative expressions, peace, light, and love come to be is a powerfully energizing yet calming experience.

Other famous meditators are Paul McCartney, Arianna Huffington, Kobe Bryant, Ellen DeGeneres, Katy Perry, Angelina Jolie, Jennifer Aniston, and more.

You will notice that as you build a meditation practice, you begin to experience bliss. Gradually, you will want to meditate for longer periods just because you feel better. Other benefits of meditating are that your thoughts become clearer, you feel more peaceful, you are less reactive, and you can find solutions to every problem.

As you find this new way of being, people will wonder what is different about you. You will look younger, you will feel peaceful, and you will be more insightful and have a sharper mind. There is no need to explain. Just enjoy the benefits of your own doing.

A daily meditation practice is utterly life-changing. It can be challenging at first to sit in stillness and quiet our restless "monkey minds."

Meditation and Science

For years, I was a crisis meditator. I would go days or weeks without meditating until something bad happened, and then I would go back to meditate. I would feel the difference in myself.

After a while, I was able to link my well-being with the practice of meditation. I became less reactive and more centered. I could make decisions with ease and hear the guidance available about everything. Of course, I fought much of the guidance I received because I wanted to do something different. The times I didn't follow it, I learned my lesson.

There is a wealth of scientific studies that confirm what yogis have known for centuries: meditation dramatically reduces stress, increases focus and emotional intelligence, boosts immunity, promotes greater compassion, enhances sleep quality, and more.

In my mid-twenties, I had very low emotional intelligence. When I got to my forties, my emotional intelligence improved drastically with no intentional effort. The only activity I did was to meditate.

On a spiritual level, by calming our thoughts, we gain crystal clear access to what we already know, in addition to inner wisdom, intuition, and higher guidance that profoundly shapes our destiny. Meditation is like taking a deep soul bath, cleansing limiting thoughts so we can align with our truth. Meditation will open the path for you to remember your purpose, if you don't know it yet, and clarify the steps you need to take.

Don't worry about "doing it right." Simply start where you are.

CHAPTER 3:

ASK FOR HELP

> Asking for help is an act of
> generosity and kindness.

The third tool to help you embrace your successful self is to learn to ask for help without guilt, shame, or regret. You don't have to do everything. I know you can, but there is no need to. People have a hard time asking for help. Some women expect others to read their minds and offer assistance without being asked. They don't want to feel rejected. Men don't ask for help because they have been conditioned to be the ones who give help.

Then, we have another superhuman group of men and women who don't ask for help because they need to control everything and believe no one has the capacity to perform better, faster, or neater than they would. Which category are you in?

Somehow, asking for help became a sign of weakness when it's an opportunity to be generous. But some people view it as an opportunity to be rejected.

Here is a new thought: What if asking for help was an opportunity for the people in our lives to practice kindness? That would be our chance to allow others to be generous with their time and effort and help us. In a way, asking for help is an act of self-generosity and kindness for the people who help us.

My experience has been that many people don't know how to ask for help. Some people shower in resentment for weeks, months, and years and blame others for not helping when help was never asked. These are old paradigms that deny our sacred interconnectedness. I don't know about you, but 99.9% of the people I know don't have crystal balls and cannot read minds. If you need help, just ask.

Asking for help is not difficult. First, use the phrase "would you" every time you ask someone to help. Second, detach from the outcome. If people say yes or no, it is their decision, not yours. Third, don't extend the event. Their reasoning for saying yes or no is none of your concern. If they helped you, great; and if they didn't, find someone else. Our ancestors did it so well that they brought humanity forward.

Understanding that we are propagating generosity when asking for help is a fundamental change in the mindset. Just ask, and you will see how generous people can be with their time and effort. When we build on our ability to ask for help, we spread more generosity into our lives and into the world.

The best way to overcome limiting beliefs around asking for help is just by asking for help. When asking feels uncomfortable, remember all that you have graciously done for others. If you have not, then it's time to do your part. Seeing help as circulating energy also takes pressure off both parties. No one is above or beneath help.

If no one seems available to assist you, allow the Universe to do Its job. Sometimes, we must grow the muscle of radical self-reliance before others can step forward. You may then inspire your self-growth. Be patient with your own and other people's evolution.

Generosity and Kindness

Many women often put themselves last, thinking they can do it all. But putting on your own oxygen mask first is key to having the energy to serve others. The world needs YOUR unique talents.

Honor the flow of life. It's the dichotomy of balance. We see it so often that we may have learned to take it for granted. There is night and day, up and down, small and large, health and sickness, so ***give and receive***.

CHAPTER 4:

TRUST YOUR INTUITION

> Intuition is a real superpower.

Intuition is women's superpower. Men have intuition, too, but they tend not to hear it, while women hear it more often but don't always follow it. The fourth tool to help you embrace your success and improve your life is to trust your intuition.

Intuition is that inner knowing that no one can explain. We all have wisdom and inner guidance that helps us move in the direction of truth. The big question is how we know the voice we hear is our intuition.

Take 5 seconds and count from 1 to 5 in your head. 1, 2, 3, 4, 5. That's what the voice of intuition sounds like. Yes, just like that. Do it again. Count 1 to 10 in your head. This time, pay attention to the tone and emotions. 1, 2, 3, 4, 5, 6, 7, 8, 9, 10.

The voice of intuition is non-threatening and non-critical. It surfaces like a light nudge. There is a sense of peace and encouragement in what we are guided to do.

Just like you know that number 4 came after number 3, this sense of knowing is available for everything in our life when we learn to hear the voice of our intuition.

Meditation will also increase your connection with your intuitive self. The key is to start paying attention to your intuition, and it will become louder and repetitive. The more you follow that guidance, the more you will be able to call on it when you need it.

Learning to trust this wise inner voice is crucial to unlocking your full potential. Intuition is like an ever-present friend whispering guidance to navigate life gracefully.

Have you ever had a "gut feeling" that turned out to be right? This was your intuition. It arises spontaneously like a gentle breeze, usually through sensations or quick thoughts directing you to take or avoid action. But we often override this inner voice with conditioned patterns of fear, doubt, or overthinking.

Creating a sacred space, meditating, and asking your inner guidance for help will improve your attention to your intuition. The more you act on your intuitive hits - which simply means following through on positive impulses - the stronger this inner channel grows. Intuition celebrates action.

I, too, have ignored my intuition, but these days, when it is leading me to take a different direction than I want, I ask it again, just like counting in my head. Often, I ask if this guidance is coming from me or them, my inner guidance. And I hear the answer. Too many times, I wanted something so bad, or I was stressed out, and I didn't have the energy level for my intuition to come through. There were times when this guidance told me to take a nap, take a shower, meditate, or ask it the next morning because I was too far apart from the ideal connection for it to come through.

Be mindful of using your intuition for every little and unimportant thing. You don't need to ask your intuition if you should take a bath today or drink water or soda. You are in this world to physically live and experience the world. Don't abuse your intuition, and don't give up your power.

I have reconciled this balance by asking my intuition to warn me multiple times if I am missing something important. The biggest detriment to working with your intuition is fear and stress. When you feel fear or stress, you disconnect yourself from the Universal Mind that encompasses all that there is. Often, what we think is our intuition is the voice of a parent, teacher, or someone who influenced us based on their own fears.

For example, as a child, you read tons of books, and one day, you express your desire to become a writer. Your uncle Bob immediately discouraged you by saying, "Writers make no money! Do you want to be poor and live on the streets? Stop that nonsense, and go be a lawyer. Lawyers make good money. You are very smart, and you could be a good lawyer." No child wants to live on the street, so the image of being poor becomes an imprint in the subconscious of the child.

Every child wants to be liked, and early on, they learn to please adults. The surprising comment from Uncle Bob can make an impact on anyone, especially if you really like Uncle Bob. His fears may rise up next time you feel called to do something about your love for writing.

Meditation will help you clear the false, fearful voices in your head. Also, the best aid to improving your intuition is taking action. If you remember wanting to be a writer and receive guidance to take writing classes, act on it.

It may take a few tries before you fully pay attention to your intuition about writing, painting, starting your own business, leaving your marriage, changing jobs, or anything you have been called to. Just relax because your intuition never gives up on you. Also, If you ignored the guidance you received but later understood it was an opportunity, let it pass. You still have time to acknowledge it. Just say, "I will pay attention next time." Also, if you followed the guidance, which paid off for you, say "Thank you."

Your intuition is a spiritual muscle. Use it to improve it. As your intuition strengthens, you will feel divinely guided, confident, and free to blossom and improve your life.

CHAPTER 5:

BE IN TIMEFULNESS

> You cannot manage Time,
> but you can align yourself with it.

Our thoughts are powerful creators. Nowhere is this truer than with our relationship to time. This chapter will teach you about Tool #5, Be in Timefulness, as the new Time Management.

The present moment is all that exists - yet we continually sacrifice the "now" for a mirage. This Timefulness tool is about renewing your beliefs about time. Let's learn how to inhabit each precious moment fully.

When it comes to "Time," you need to know two concepts:

1) You have as much time as you think you do, and

2) You need to schedule downtime to have more time.

How Much Time Do You Really Have?

When you say, "I'm too busy," "I don't have enough time," or "I work too much," you affirm a life of not enough time and plenty of stress. You also create additional tasks for your already full schedule when you say these affirmations because they become your truth.

I am not implying that you quit working, stop your education, neglect your family, or ditch your parents to make more time. Let's change the framework. Start affirming that you have as much time as you need to do what is important to you, and that includes downtime to enjoy life.

This is not about just thinking positive when your days are long and your tasks endless. I used to think I was too busy, that I worked too much, and that I didn't have enough time for myself. That's the reality I created.

I always thought about work. I received calls on my days off, and I worked longer days and even during vacations. The more I complained, the busier I was. The busier I was, the more I complained. Do you see the pattern? My "no time" life-affirmation created a self-fulfilling prophecy.

I also used to believe that I didn't have time to write and that I could only write on my days off. That's not true. The moment I changed my relationship with time and was fully committed to writing, I had plenty of time to write, even with a career that required me to be on call seven days a week.

I first connected the dots when I had doctor's appointments for my children. I usually set up doctor's appointments early in the morning or late in the day. One day, I was running 30 minutes late. I didn't want to call the office because I was afraid they would tell me to reschedule it. I was speeding through the streets, blowing yellow/red lights and stop signs, and holding my gaze at the clock as if it would slow time.

I parked horribly outside the one assigned spot and yanked my children out of the car. I held my youngest and pulled my oldest to the elevator door like a storm was coming. I hit the elevator button multiple times to speed it up, but they don't hurry because I am in a hurry. I arrived at the doctor's desk sweating like a lunatic – my speed only yielded 2 minutes off. I was now 28 minutes late.

I quickly mumbled something about the traffic apologetically to the clerk and pulled out my insurance card after shuffling it in my purse. The clerk looked at me like I had three heads and said calmly, "Ms. Barreto, the doctor is running late this afternoon; it will be about 45 minutes before he can see the girls. There are three people ahead of you. Have a seat; we will call you when he is ready."

It turned out that I had plenty of time. Thinking that I didn't have time created more stress than it called for it. Because I believed I didn't have enough time to meet my obligations, every minute was a stressful one, and I didn't have access to all the time management intelligence I knew.

It's time for everyone to have a renewed relationship with time. Mine started with an affirmation: I have as much time as I think I do. I have as much time as I think I do.

When I began working on my time affirmation, I didn't believe I had plenty of time, but I affirmed it anyway. I repeat these words every time I feel I am rushing. And there is an immediate feeling of release and calm in my mind and body. I feel my shoulders drop immediately, and a deeper breath follows. I accept where I am in my time, and all is well.

I used to over-schedule, over-commit myself, and set aggressive goals. I accomplished most of those goals but at the cost of my health, happiness, and presence in life. I learned that stress is an expensive car that you pay for but don't drive or own.

I encourage you to change your relationship with time today. Start with writing an affirmation. Please do it now. Pause and don't delay. This will be a game change for you.

Now that you have your affirmation place it on your bathroom mirror, set daily affirmation alerts on your phone to remind you throughout your day, and place a post-it note on your computer or the dashboard of your car. You will see how much time you have.

Create More Time

The second time concept to learn is "You need to schedule downtime to have more time;" I know it sounds counterintuitive, but it is true. Your mind thinks that if you schedule downtime, you will do less. Then you will be stressed because things won't be completed, right?

This is erroneous thinking.

If you have been too busy, you have created a habit of crossing accomplishments, big or small. You may have become Dopamine addicted. You will know if you feel compelled to check your phone each time it dings, and you must clear the number of alerts on your screen all the time or open every email as they come. It's a habit, and you can unlearn it.

Dopamine motivates people to take action. It's not all bad, but too much activity will get you out of sorts and too busy to enjoy your life.

It's time to schedule downtimes. It will not extend the 1,440 minutes you have in the day, but it will expand your accomplishments and possibilities.

Your words program your subconscious mind and directly shape your reality. It guides you to act in a certain way. You manifest exactly what you think is possible. The more you believe you are too busy, the more overwhelmed you will feel. You remember all the work you had when you returned from vacation, right?

This time management hack works. Instead of doing all the work ahead so you can plan the time off, schedule the downtime ahead every week and trust the Universe will show up. I am asking you to schedule it because you may become too busy to do it.

When you give yourself time, time expands to accommodate your needs. You become so accepting of what happens that solutions just come into your experience. You leave unfinished work behind, and the work gets done, or you have a better solution, an easier way to do it when you come back. Basically, you become accepting of the worst-case scenario (from your head) that never happens, and in the process, you give yourself more loving care.

Pause now and observe how much you defer living while waiting for some future event such as more income, perfect relationship, familial duty, retirement, or vacation. All conditions will eventually change. If not now, when? This moment is guaranteed; the future never is. Fully step and inhabit your now and schedule your first downtime today.

I have noticed that many people who think they lack time only lack discipline and clarity. You may spend hours scrolling social media or aimlessly watching TV, yet claim no time for exercise, nourishing food, or relationships. Please don't fault yourself. It's likely the result of not being happy. When you spend all of your time doing what you" have to do" instead of what you "would love to do," you lose energy for joy.

This is the time to be radically honest. You do have time; just be clear about your priorities. Closely assess how you spend time. When you embrace Timefulness, you:

- Schedule commitments consciously

- Block off sacred rest, play, and creativity times.

- Set firm boundaries.

- Say "no" without guilt.

Your life must align with your soul's purpose. Flow with each day organically rather than packing it full.

Explore savoring nourishing activities like walks, reading, hot baths, and lovemaking. By honoring your need for relaxation and inspiration, you gain the energy to accomplish goals fueled by passion versus duty. Detach from arbitrary timelines; trust your immutable inner clock.

Be in Timefulness; that's where you and your soul play in the sand of happiness.

Chapter 6:

CULTIVATE GRATITUDE

> Giving thanks at least 10 times
> a day keeps unhappiness away.

What is the word people use when they receive a gift, a compliment, or a nice gesture? THANK YOU. "Thank you" is an after-action: we receive, and then we give thanks. Our minds automatically spell out our Gratitude through feelings, words, and emotions. We habitually feel appreciated by simple actions such as having a door opened for us, being handed something we dropped, or greater things like receiving a kidney.

The sixth tool to support you in embracing your success is Gratitude. When you feel Gratitude, the mind feels safe. There is no resistance. When we feel safe, we have more physical, emotional, and mindful resources available to us. We become our best selves.

It is impossible for you to feel grateful and fearful, angry, resentful, or any negative emotion at the same time. So what if we could reverse the process? What if we could give thanks and then receive? What if we could feel Gratitude before the moment? We can.

Our brain doesn't know that we have not yet received appreciation because it receives signals from our emotions. If thought alone can make the body feel stressed, it can also make the body feel grateful and all of the positive emotions that accompany Gratitude. And all we need to do is to think about the people, things, and events that we are grateful for even before it happens.

Gratitude is the most powerful tool you can have in your life. Having a daily practice of Gratitude will improve your mood and your relationships with everything. I mean "Everything!" Your outlook on life will be more positive. Most of all, when you start practicing Gratitude, just by being grateful for the small things, the Universe will deliver to you more things to be grateful for.

Here is a suggestion. When you first wake up in the morning, before you look at your clock or your phone, or even before going to the bathroom, find five things to be grateful for. It is nice to start with your bed, your pillows, your room, and your home. If you don't like your home, think of the people who are sleeping in a hut. When you do, your home becomes a palace, and it is easier to appreciate.

At night, as you go to bed before you fall asleep, comb through your day and find five things to be grateful for. Your job, the toll collector, the nice dinner, the fruit you ate for breakfast, anything that you can be grateful for. But don't stop at five if you can. We could be giving thanks ten times a day every day to boost our health, relationships, happiness, and connection with a higher power.

Our minds have become accustomed to paying attention to what is missing instead of what we have. Somehow, we learn to complain, be offended by, and point fingers at what our personalities think is absent. Gratitude has been high-jacked by the bad attitude. We complain about the pollen of the spring, the heat of the summer, the wind of the fall, and the cold of the winter. And yet, we need the seasons to be in balance.

If you don't like your job, find 10 things you can appreciate about your job. If you don't like your spouse, find ten grateful moments you shared together in the past. If you don't like your family, find ten qualities you could appreciate about them. I know some of you may need to use a magnifying glass, but it's a beginning. When you begin a practice of Gratitude, appreciation comes in tenfold.

These moments of Gratitude change how you think, feel, and act. You will have access to the best self and act with love and kindness.

I am not suggesting that you stay in an abusive relationship or miserable working conditions. This practice of finding Gratitude is not pretending that everything is wine and roses. However, it will catapult you to take the best action instead of overreacting or caving in. Gratitude helps you act with grace.

Pay attention to the days when your boss is on your case, your business has a setback, your children are driving you crazy, or you are not too happy with your partner. Find 10 things to appreciate about them, and you will release that resistance that magnifies unhappiness. It will reset your emotions and help you handle your issues with the best version of yourself at that moment.

I noticed that when I find appreciation for an area of my life that is not working as I would like, those events or people either disappear or improve when I find drops of Gratitude around my life.

The Practice

As you go through your day, be mindful of things to appreciate. When I am driving and I see birds, I am reminded to be thankful. Then, I name something I can be grateful for at that moment. In the fall, when flocks of birds fly by, I know that the Universe is working with me. Feel free to use the birds, but you can use butterflies, flowers, or anything that makes you happy.

You could also use Gratitude when you have a work issue. Find at least 10 things to appreciate, and if the work becomes tough, try 20.

Your Job and Gratitude

Gratitude is more powerful than most people think. Please pay close attention here if you want to change jobs. It's best to mend any strong emotions about your job with Gratitude, or the right job for you can't come if you don't appreciate the job you have. And if you manage to willpower your way to a new job, you are very likely to experience the same issues from your previous job. The same thing happens with romantic relationships, homes, and money.

If you want to leave the past behind, begin to appreciate aspects of your previous one. Use Gratitude to clear your emotions and leave the past behind. Oh, I forgot to tell you that it's free, free, free.

Now you know why some people keep dating the same person over and over or change jobs with the same complaints. Gratitude is the healing tool everyone needs to move forward.

If you feel it is hard to appreciate the person who cheated on you, left you without warning, or stole from you, begin softening your heart and find honest Gratitude for the struggle you experienced. By intentionally cultivating daily gratitude practices, you alchemize pain into joy, lack into abundance, and annoying moments into blessings.

Gratitude is that long breath we release when we feel safe. Find it at least 10 times a day and watch the quality of your life improve like endless waves.

CHAPTER 7:

LETTING GO

> Letting go is an act of trust that everything will always work out.

Friends, are you holding on to people, things, and emotions that need to go? If your answer is "no," how do you really know?

Nothing is permanent in life. Everything is always evolving. We have hours, days, weeks, and seasons. When it is time to transition into something new, your old ways stop working. So look at everything that is not working in your life and ask yourself if it is time to let some things go.

In this chapter, we will explore your level of attachment to things, people, and emotions and how letting go improves the quality of your life.

The biggest clue you have to understand where you are with attachment is to look at clutter. One of my good friends has too many objects in her house. She doesn't call it clutter because she just loves each one of them, even the ones that are in boxes, and she doesn't use them.

So, close your eyes and take three deep breaths before reading the next sentence.

Are there areas of your home that could benefit from decluttering? Is it your closet or garage? Is it the spare room or the attic? Or are you keeping storage units to hide from yourself that you may have a problem?

Clutter is a lack of trust in yourself. Read it again. When you have clutter, there is a part of you that doesn't trust yourself. It may have happened so long ago that you may not remember. It's painful to go back and examine the emotions that led you to believe that someday you may not have enough or don't feel you are enough now. This is not true. You are enough. You always have been enough, even if others made you feel incomplete. You have all the tools to create an amazing life, but the clutter is distracting the best part of you, diverting your attention to the past and holding you prisoner with low-level energies.

Clutter stops new seasons from coming. It's like you are living in a perpetual winter of life. You are missing the spring, summer, and fall.

People with clutter in their homes are likely to hold on to past emotions and people who no longer contribute positively to their lives.

How to Begin?

Start where you are with what you have. The less challenging way to let go is to begin in the bedroom. Be patient and find a friend to help you. Once, I worked with a client who was a stay-at-home mom of a teenager in her mid-forties and needed my help to return to work and redirect her career and life.

When we reviewed her life, she had clutter in many areas of her home. The worst was that she still had items from her previous marriage, like the bed, mattress, linen, and wardrobe. She had remarried 18 years earlier but was still holding on to the past. When you are ready for change, you must let go of the past.

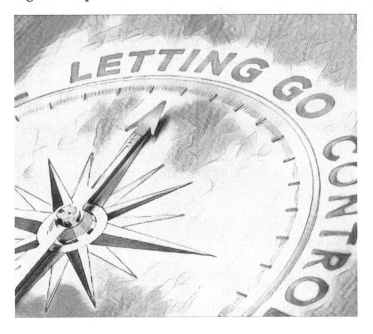

We set small goals to begin clearing her bedroom of clutter because she didn't feel motivated to do much in the house. She struggled to do simple tasks, so I gave her small tasks each week. I asked to start with the shoes she didn't use anymore and old clothes she didn't like, even if they were family gifts. Because the energy of her home was too draining, it took her three weeks to get clothes out of the wardrobe and into the hallways to be donated. In the fourth week, her husband removed everything under the bed even though she didn't ask him. Once she cleaned the clutter in her bedroom, she had more energy to follow the steps for her career.

Do yourself a favor, set a day today to remove the clutter from your home, and start with your bedroom. If something is broken, throw it away or fix it today. If you don't like it or it is not being used, sell it or donate it today. Get all the unlikable gifts you received as a present and re-gift or donate them. A clutter hack I strongly recommend is to get the bags of donations or garbage out of the home immediately. The trash goes to the garage, and the donation goes into the front seat of your car, so you don't forget about it. If you don't drive, it will go into the front seat of your friend's car.

When you let go, you create more space in your home, mind, and spirit. This is prime real estate in your life. Do a walk-through every three months and find things to de-clutter. This will help release other things and emotions that diminish your attention and peace.

Trust yourself. Everything you need will come at the right time if you believe it.

CHAPTER 8:

SHARE YOUR GIFTS

> You are the gift.

Tool number eight is for you to share your natural gifts. Everyone has a gift for the world, no exceptions. Everyone has a unique way of contributing to humanity. When you weigh happiness, contribution to the world rates very high, if not the #1 happiness fact. You don't have to be Emily Dickinson, who gifted us inspiration, or Princess Isabel, who freed the enslaved people in Brazil to contribute. Everyone, from stay-at-home mothers to CEOs, has a gift to give to the world. And you are no different regardless of where you are in the stage of life.

Have you heard of Grandma Moses? Her real name was Anna Mary Robertson Moses. She was born in 1860 and lived on a rural farm in upstate New York, about 50 minutes from my home. As a young woman, she worked hard doing chores and household duties, leaving little time for artistic pursuits. When she found the courage to share her gifts, she was 78 years old. She became a painter, a very famous one.

After her husband passed away, Grandma Moses picked up embroidery. Then she moved on to painting scenes of rural American life using whatever materials she could find - oils, varnish, house paints on canvas or wood. Her paintings captured the simple pleasures and hard work of farm life in a naive, folksy style.

In 1938, at age 78, an art collector discovered her works at a drug store and was captivated by their honest charm. He ended up buying several and getting them displayed at the Museum of Modern Art in New York City. Overnight, Grandma Moses became a media sensation - her paintings graced Christmas cards and magazine covers. She even made it into a Norman Rockwell painting.

Despite her very late start, she painted furiously for over 25 years, creating over 1,500 works. Major museums and collectors clamored for her paintings. When she passed away in 1961 at age 101, Grandma Moses had achieved worldwide acclaim as one of America's most famous and successful folk artists despite women painters being overlooked.

Her life story reminds us that it's never too late to discover your talents and passions when female painters represent only 2% of the market. No matter your age or circumstances, if you have a creative gift inside yearning to come out, don't let self-doubt or fear hold you back from sharing it with the world.

What is your gift? Only you know. You may think that you don't know, but you do. Consider this book another nudge of the Universe. Life has already given you clues, and your unconscious mind has some strong opinions as to what your gift is. If you do, then step into your future. Perhaps you feel that delivering your gift to the world is too difficult, that you may be rejected, or that there is no money in it and you need to work for a living.

These life-serving gifts cannot be measured, although some people may try to. We can't quantify or qualify the gift of motherhood. A stay-at-home mother who raises a child who goes on to discover the cure for diabetes may be seen as just another mother, but she is more than that. She provided the environment for a child to flourish. A cleaning lady who cleans the house of a female entrepreneur who employs thousands of people is also sharing her gifts with the world. You need to walk into a clean house after a long day of work to appreciate the gift of a spotless home.

Recognizing Your Gifts

What brings you joy? Where do you naturally excel? Who have you been told you inspire? What skills seem effortless for you? Your soul's purpose is revealed through these clues. Even introverts have quiet gifts to share.

Be mindful of your close friend, the Ego. It distracts you with fears of unworthiness and perfectionism because it knows how to influence you. "Who are you to share this gift?" it asks. How you answer it may keep you stuck where you are instead of on the road to happiness.

More than ever, women are being called to share their gifts with the world. Some have heard the call, and others are too busy justifying their limitations with all of the reasons why they can't open that door.

Do you think that Grandma Moses expected to have her works displayed in Museums and Galleries throughout the world? Her paintings were hung in a small-town drugstore. She didn't call art critics; she just wanted to get her passion to come out of her. And the Universe rewards action.

Start small. You don't have to leave your job to begin sharing your gifts. You don't need to wait until the children are older, retire, or have enough money to leave your job. You can start today. All you need is a decision.

What thoughts have been nudging you to act? This is not a warning you heard yesterday. You now have the sacred space, a meditation practice that connects you with your inner guidance, and you know how to hear your intuition. Make a decision. You don't have to do it alone; you know how to ask for help. When you clear the clutter, you free space in your mind to start. Also, you know what is important to you and can use your time wisely. You are ready now. Actually, you have always been.

Please answer the wake-up call. Your courage is calling. Your biggest fear may be hiding from you. You may think you are afraid of failure, but you are also afraid of success. Women are more afraid of success than rejection or failure.

But what if you hit really big? What if the people doubting your abilities are wrong? What if your early training to be small and play it safe was just a deception? What if everything you heard about playing it safe in life was a family conditioning that tamed your freedom and joy?

Every day, more women are hearing the call of their spirit to open a business, get an education, march for rights, apply for promotion, run for office, and even for the Presidency of the United States. Women are called to be happy.

So, go open that business, earn your degree, get that big job, buy that house, learn how to dance, leave that marriage, and say yes to life. And when insecurity creeps back in, call on your practice of Gratitude. Remember, you cannot be fearful and grateful. Find Gratitude and watch your brave self move forward.

We need your gift. No one can do what you do, just the way you do. The more you share your gifts, the more space we create for other people to share their gifts. Walk into your season with both feet on the ground, heart and mind connected so your spirit can blossom. Share your gift with humanity. There is only one of you in the whole Universe. Celebrate!

You are the gift!

Women are the heart of humanity. When you do well, everyone around you does well, too. Your inspired life will inspire others. Embrace your success.

Chapter 9:

A NOTE OF GRATITUDE

Dear Reader, thank you for joining me on this unique journey. I hope you know in your heart that your success is your ownership of your undisputable gift: **You.**

Remember, you are never alone - we walk this winding path together. When the path seems obscured, use the tools in the book and watch your light expand; your essence remains bright, beautiful, and untouchable. As you soar, the quality of your life will improve at a quantum rate.

Keep navigating by the compass of your heart. Joy is the path that guides you to take the next step. My intention for you is that you feel empowered to integrate the eight tools we've explored in this book; they help you recognize your strengths. Regularly reflect on your progress with self-love and allow your practices to take root and blossom organically.

When you stumble or notice doubt creeping in, use one of the tools. Your intuition will tell you which one. Treat yourself softly as you would a child learning to walk. Growth is not linear. Be patient with your process of embracing your success. The light within you is eager to shine its true radiance, and it will flow naturally. I can't wait to see it!

Today, I bow to the incredible person you already are and the one you are blossoming into. May you continue shining ever more boldly as you walk your sacred path. Our world so deeply needs your light, and I wait, drenched in Gratitude for your gift to humanity.

This book is based on the Motivational Talk "Share Your Gifts" I received in meditation and recorded in 2017. It has been downloaded over 272k. As I practice Tool #3, please help me share my gift with the world by sharing it on social media, writing a review on Amazon, Barnes & Noble, and Good Reads, and buying additional copies for friends who would enjoy a short read.

ABOUT THE AUTHOR

With over 20 years of studying Transformational Leadership and self-empowerment and 30+ years of business experience spanning corporate roles and entrepreneurship, Ana Barreto is a Brazilian-American author, teacher, coach, entrepreneur, and founder of the Body, Mind & Wisdom School for Women, where she aims to help and support women on their journey to self-empowerment.

Though holding Bachelor's and Master's degrees in Business, Ana was drawn to psychology, women's history, spirituality, and Eastern wisdom. While balancing work, family, and education, she voraciously studied these topics along with leadership, well-being, and unlocking human potential.

In addition to publishing six books on personal growth topics for women, Ana's calling as a guide is to champion the unlimited potential of her readers and students. Having learned what she now writes and teaches, she embodies compassion for the unique pressures and limiting self-perception women face as they take on increased responsibilities and leadership roles. She has guided many teams and individuals in the corporate and personal sphere to boldly develop their talents while overcoming fear, imposter syndrome, or avoidance behaviors that can sabotage success.

Ana's purpose is to serve women who need confidence, support, and motivation to enhance their well-being and live to their highest potential. Through writing, teaching, coaching, meditations, and inspirational resources, she guides women to discover their inner brilliance and thrive authentically.

When not writing or working, Ana enjoys cooking, traveling, hiking, biking, kayaking, and spending time with her husband, their children, family, and friends.